CONGRATULATIONS YOU'RE A DAD

Kate Freeman

summersdale

Summersdale Publishers Ltd
46 West Street
Chichester
West Sussex
PO19 1RP
UK

www.summersdale.com

Printed and bound in the Czech Republic

ISBN: 978-1-84953-747-6

Substantial discounts on bulk quantities of Summersdale books are available to corporations, professional associations and other organisations. For details contact Nicky Douglas by telephone: +44 (0) 1243 756902, fax: +44 (0) 1243 786300 or email: nicky@summersdale.com.

To Rich

From Aunty Marion

x

A grand adventure is about to begin.

A. A. Milne

Any man can be a father, but it takes a special person to be a dad.

Anonymous

I'm 482 months old;
can you tell I'm a
new father?

Reno Goodale

**To witness
the birth of a
child is our best
opportunity to
experience the
meaning of the
word 'miracle'.**

Paul Carvel

Being a great father is like shaving. No matter how good you shaved today, you have to do it again tomorrow.

Reed Markham

My father gave me
the greatest gift
anyone could give
another person: he
believed in me.

Jim Valvano

SAY HELLO TO YOUR NEW LIFE AS 'DADA!'

**The raising of
a child is the
building of a
cathedral. You
can't cut corners.**

Dave Eggers

**When you
look at your
life the greatest
happinesses are
family happinesses.**

Joyce Brothers

**Life doesn't come
with an instruction
book; that's why we
have fathers.**

H. Jackson Brown Jr

A baby is God's opinion that the world should go on.

Carl Sandburg

Great oaks
from little
acorns grow.

Anonymous

Anyone who tells you fatherhood is the greatest thing that can happen to you, they are understating it.

Mike Myers

HELLO,
2 A.M.!

A baby is an inestimable blessing and bother.

Mark Twain

People who say they sleep like a baby usually don't have one.

Leo J. Burke

**Children
reinvent your
world for you.**

Susan Sarandon

Babies are always more trouble than you thought – and more wonderful.

Charles Osgood

What do I owe my father? Everything.

Henry Van Dyke

I'm not going to
have a better day,
a more magical
moment, than the
first time I heard
my daughter giggle.

Sean Penn

HAVE YOU GOT THE BOTTLE?

Getting a burp out of your little thing is probably the greatest satisfaction I've come across.

Brad Pitt

**There are times
when parenthood
seems nothing but
feeding the mouth
that bites you.**

Peter De Vries

Did you know babies are nauseated by the smell of a clean shirt?

Jeff Foxworthy

Dads grab
themselves a spoon
and dig right in
with you.

Anonymous

I've made a few nice dishes in my time, but this has got to be the best one I've ever made.

Jamie Oliver talking about his first child

**The only rock I
know that stays
steady, the only
institution I know
that works, is
the family.**

Lee Iacocca

A LIE-IN –
WHAT'S THAT?

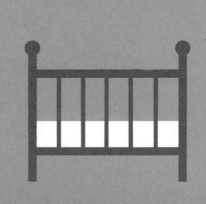

A perfect example of minority rule is a baby in the house.

Anonymous

Each day of our lives we make deposits in the memory banks of our children.

Charles R. Swindoll

You can learn
many things from
children. How much
patience you have,
for instance.

Franklin P. Jones

If your children look up to you, you've made a success of life's biggest job.

Anonymous

Other things may
change us, but we
start and end
with family.

Anthony Brandt

The family is one of nature's masterpieces.

George Santayana

THIS LITTLE PIGGY WENT TO MARKET...

Children learn to smile from their parents.

Shinichi Suzuki

You will always be your child's favourite toy.

Vicki Lansky

One's family is the most important thing in life.

Robert Byrd

Children make your life important.

Erma Bombeck

My father was my
teacher. But most
importantly he
was a great dad.

Beau Bridges

One of the things that binds us as a family is a shared sense of humour.

Ralph Fiennes

NOW YOU'RE A BABYGROW PRO!

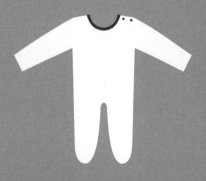

A father is a man who expects his children to be as good as he meant to be.

Frank A. Clark

Nothing you do for children is ever wasted.

Garrison Keillor

The most valuable thing you can spend on your children is time.

Anonymous

**To a young boy,
the father is a
giant from whose
shoulders you can
see for ever.**

Perry Garfinkel

Fathers embody a delicious mixture of familiarity and novelty. They are novel without being strange or frightening.

Louise J. Kaplan

For many people, God is just Dad with a mask on.

Anonymous

SLEEP?
I REMEMBER THAT...

Having children gives your life a purpose. Right now, my purpose is to get some sleep.

Reno Goodale

No animal is so inexhaustible as an excited infant.

Amy Leslie

The secret of fatherhood is to know when to stop tickling.

Anonymous

Always kiss your children goodnight, even if they're already asleep.

H. Jackson Brown Jr

I loved my father.
I looked for his
faithful response
in the eyes of
many men.

Patricia Neal

Govern a family
as you would
cook a small fish –
very gently.

Chinese proverb

SHAKE, RATTLE AND ROLL!

**The quickest way
for a parent to get
a child's attention
is to sit down and
look comfortable.**

Lane Olinghouse

When you are dealing with a child, keep all your wits about you, and sit on the floor.

Austin O'Malley

You don't have to deserve your mother's love. You have to deserve your father's. He's more particular.

Robert Frost

The quality of a
father can be seen
in the goals, dreams
and aspirations he
sets not only for
himself, but for
his family.

Reed Markham

While we try to teach our children all about life, our children teach us what life is all about.

Angela Schwindt

**Even when
freshly washed
and relieved of all
obvious confections,
children tend to
be sticky.**

Fran Lebowitz

IT'S NURSERY RHYME TIME!

Before I got married I had six theories about bringing up children; now I have six children and no theories.

*John Wilmot,
2nd Earl of Rochester*

Good fathers make good sons.

Anonymous

Family is not an important thing. It's everything.

Michael J. Fox

Blessed indeed is the man who hears many gentle voices call him father!

Lydia Maria Child

Dads regard
themselves as giant
shock absorbers,
there to protect the
family from the
ruts and bumps on
the road of life.

W. Bruce Cameron

When my father
didn't have my
hand... he had
my back.

Linda Poindexter

IT'S BYE-BYE
SPORTS CAR,
HELLO
FAMILY CAR.

It goes without saying that you should never have more children than you have car windows.

Erma Bombeck

A father is a banker provided by nature.

French proverb

Always try to be a little kinder than is necessary.

J. M. Barrie

A good father is one of the most unsung, unpraised, unnoticed, and yet one of the most valuable assets in our society.

Billy Graham

I looked up to my dad. He was always on a ladder.

Anonymous

My father used to say that it's never too late to do anything you wanted to do.

Michael Jordan

WONDER
HOW TO GET INTO DRAWERS ONCE THE HOME
HAS BEEN BABY-PROOFED?

My father gave me the greatest gift anyone could give another person: he believed in me.

Jim Valvano

Children are not a distraction from more important work. They are the most important work.

C. S. Lewis

I cannot think
of any need in
childhood as strong
as the need for a
father's protection.

Sigmund Freud

My best training came from my father.

Woodrow Wilson

He opened the jar of pickles when no one else could.

Erma Bombeck on her dad

Dad taught me everything I know. Unfortunately, he didn't teach me everything he knows.

Al Unser Jr

IT MUST BE
NAP TIME.

There's no pillow quite so soft as a father's strong shoulder.

Richard L. Evans

Anyone who thinks the art of conversation is dead ought to tell a child to go to bed.

Robert Gallagher

There's no road map on how to raise a family: it's always an enormous negotiation.

Meryl Streep

I cannot understand
how in the past I
managed to cope
without getting
cuddled this many
times a day.

Russell Crowe

**Nothing could get
at me if I curled up
on my father's lap...
All about him
was safe.**

Naomi Mitchison

You don't choose
your family.
They are God's gift
to you, as you
are to them.

Desmond Tutu

HERE'S ONE FOR THE FAMILY ALBUM.

To us, family means putting your arms around each other and being there.

Barbara Bush

Noble fathers have noble children.

Euripides

A truly rich man is
one whose children
run into his arms
when his hands
are empty.

Anonymous

I don't mind looking into the mirror and seeing my father.

Michael Douglas

By the time a man realises his father was right, he has a son who thinks he's wrong.

Charles Wadsworth

Rejoice with your family in the beautiful land of life.

Albert Einstein

FUN PLUS ONE.

My dad's probably one of the kindest people in the world.

Leonardo DiCaprio

**Fathering is not
something perfect
men do, but
something that
perfects the man.**

Frank Pittman

Having one child
makes you a parent;
having two makes
you a referee.

David Frost

A father is someone you look up to, no matter how tall you are.

Anonymous

Your dad is the man
who does all the
heavy shovelling
for your sandcastle,
and then tells
you you've done a
wonderful job.

Rose O'Kelly

There are three stages of a man's life: he believes in Santa Claus, he doesn't believe in Santa Claus, he is Santa Claus.

Anonymous

START PRACTISING YOUR SANTA STYLE.

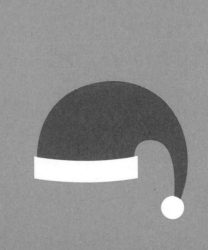

The best investment is to go home from work early and spend the afternoon throwing a ball around with your son.

Ben Stein

A happy family is but an earlier heaven.

George Bernard Shaw

A father is someone
who carries
pictures in his
wallet where his
money used to be.

Anonymous

If you want your children to listen, try talking softly – to someone else.

Ann Landers

My dad has always taught me these words: care and share.

Tiger Woods

A father's words are like a thermostat that sets the temperature in the house.

Paul Lewis

YOU ARE
THE NEW
ENCYCLOPEDIA.

I believe that what
we become depends
on what our fathers
teach us at odd
moments, when they
aren't trying to
teach us.

Umberto Eco

A person soon learns how little he knows when a child begins to ask questions.

Richard L. Evans

Parents can only advise their children or point them in the right direction.

Anne Frank

I talk and talk and talk, and I haven't taught people in fifty years what my father taught by example in one week.

Mario Cuomo

You can't
understand it until
you experience the
simple joy of the
first time your son
points at a seagull
and says 'duck'.

Russell Crowe on fatherhood

Jarrell was not so much my father... as an affectionate encyclopedia.

Mary Jarrell

LIFE'S A WALK IN THE PARK.

Your children need your presence more than your presents.

Jesse Jackson

Only a father doesn't begrudge his son's talent.

Johann Wolfgang von Goethe

I set the bar at half of my dad. If I could get that far, I'd consider my life successful.

Jeb Bush

Being a dad is more important than football.

David Beckham

If you can give
your son or
daughter only
one gift, let it
be enthusiasm.

Bruce Barton

We all knew
Dad was in charge:
he had control
of the remote.

Anonymous

SUPERDAD!

My dad is my hero.
I'm never free of a
problem nor do
I truly experience
a joy until we
share it.

Nancy Sinatra

A father's solemn
duty is to watch
football with his
children and teach
them when to shout
at the ref.

Paul Collins

The toughest job in the world isn't being a president. It's being a parent.

Bill Clinton

I love my father
as the stars – he's
a bright shining
example and a
happy twinkling
in my heart.

Adabella Radici

**Setting too good
an example is a
kind of slander
seldom forgiven.**

Benjamin Franklin

No man I ever met was my father's equal, and I never loved any other man as much.

Hedy Lamarr

HERE'S TO YOUR NEW ADVENTURE!

Children must be taught how to think, not what to think.

Margaret Mead

**Every father
should remember
that one day his
son will follow his
example instead of
his advice.**

Anonymous

There are only two lasting bequests we can hope to give our children. One of these is roots. The other, wings.

Hodding Carter

No love is greater than that of a father for his son.

Dan Brown

If you're interested in finding out more about our books, find us on Facebook at **Summersdale Publishers** and follow us on Twitter at @Summersdale.

www.summersdale.com